E-mail Security

E-mail Security

A Pocket Guide

STEVEN FURNELL
PAUL DOWLAND

it gp™

IT Governance Publishing

IT Governance Publishing
IT Governance Limited
Unit 3, Clive Court
Bartholomew's Walk
Cambridgeshire Business Park
Ely
Cambridgeshire
CB7 4EH
United Kingdom

www.itgovernance.co.uk

First published in the United Kingdom in 2010 by IT Governance Publishing.

ISBN 978-1-84928-096-9

PREFACE

E-mail is now an established and increasingly essential channel of business and personal communication. As such, safeguarding its operation and integrity is an issue of widespread significance. At the same time, e-mail has proven itself to represent a considerable threat vector, providing a route for a variety of attacks including malware, phishing and spam. In addition, e-mail usage can introduce further risks if not appropriately guided and managed, with the potential for confidentiality to be compromised and reputations to be damaged. With these points in mind it is relevant for all stakeholders to consider their role in protecting e-mail and using the service appropriately.

This guide provides a concise reference to the main security issues affecting those that deploy and use e-mail to support their organisations, considering e-mail in terms of its significance in a business context, and focusing upon why effective security policy and safeguards are crucial in ensuring the viability of business operations. The resulting coverage encompasses issues of relevance to end-users, business managers and technical staff, and this holistic approach is intended to give each key audience an understanding of the actions relevant to them, as well as an appreciation of the issues facing the other groups.

ABOUT THE AUTHORS

Professor Steven Furnell has a significant track record in information security, through both personal research and consultancy activity and via supervised PhD and Masters projects within the Centre for Security, Communications and Network Research at the University of Plymouth. He has authored more than 210 refereed papers in international journals and conferences, as well as a variety of commissioned journal articles, book chapters and books. Specific examples of the latter include *Cybercrime: Vandalising the Information Society,* Addison Wesley, Harlow, Essex (2001), *Computer Insecurity: Risking the System,* Springer, London (2005) and *Mobile Security: A Pocket Guide,* IT Governance Publishing, Ely, Cambs (2009).

Dr Paul Dowland has firsthand practical experience of administering and securing e-mail services in his role supporting the Centre for Security, Communications and Network Research at the University of Plymouth, as well as teaching both network- and application-level security principles and practice at undergraduate and postgraduate levels. He has also authored/edited more than 70 publications including 34 peer-reviewed papers in journals and international conferences.

Further details of the Centre for Security, Communications and Network Research can be found at: *www.plymouth.ac.uk/cscan*.

ACKNOWLEDGEMENTS

Dedicated to the memory of Lena Furnell ... quite a fan of e-mail in her later years!

CONTENTS

GLOSSARY OF ABBREVIATIONS

3G	3rd Generation
AV	Anti-virus
CAPTCHA	Completely Automated Public Turing test to tell Computers and Humans Apart
CC	Carbon Copy
DNS	Domain Name System
GPG	GNU Privacy Guard
HTML	HyperText Markup Language
HTTP	HyperText Transfer Protocol
HTTPS	HyperText Transfer Protocol Secure
IMAP	Internet Message Access Protocol
IP	Internet Protocol
ISP	Internet Service Provider
MD5	Message-Digest algorithm 5
MP3	MPEG-1 or MPEG-2 Audio Layer 3
MTA	Message Transfer Agent
MX	Message eXchange
NDR	Non Delivery Report
PDA	Personal Digital Assistant
PDF	Portable Document Format
PGP	Pretty Good Privacy
POP	Post Office Protocol
S/MIME	Secure/Multipurpose Internet Mail Extensions
SMTP	Simple Mail Transfer Protocol
SPF	Sender Policy Framework
SSL	Secure Sockets Layer
TCP	Transmission Control Protocol
TLS	Transport Layer Security
UA	User Agent
UBE	Unsolicited Bulk E-mail
URL	Uniform Resource Locator
USB	Universal Serial Bus
WLAN	Wireless Local Area Network

CHAPTER 1: E-MAIL: CAN WE LIVE WITHOUT IT?

E-mail fulfils an important role in modern organisations in terms of facilitating both internal communications and external relationships. However, while it offers indisputable benefits, such significant use introduces inevitable elements of dependence and exposure. Indeed, from a business perspective, the mere fact that we now place such reliance upon e-mail can introduce the first element of risk, especially when the underlying technology does not provide a guaranteed service.

It would be no exaggeration to suggest that e-mail is now the lifeblood of modern business communications. Indeed, it is conceivable that some readers may not even have experienced the pre-e-mail era, when the only options for circulating a document involved photocopying it and/or faxing it, and when memos were sent on paper (and when a cc'd recipient may in fact have received a genuine carbon copy). At the time of writing, these other modes of communication have not entirely disappeared, but they are far less commonplace and there are likely to be few modern business environments in which they are now dominant.

It is now not uncommon to find individuals who routinely receive hundreds of e-mails per day. (Whether they reply to them all is another matter!). Indeed, findings from Radicati Group suggest that business users in 2009 received an average of 74 messages per day, plus sent an average of 34 of their own, and consequently spent 19% of their working day engaged in e-mail-related activities.[1] To give this some context, the overall figure of 108 messages per day was actually down on the figure for 2008, when respondents had dealt with an average of 140 messages per day. Radicati's analysis attributed the reduction to an accompanying increase in the business use

---

[1] Radicati. 2009. *Business User Survey, 2009 – Executive Summary.* Radicati Group Inc., November 2009.

of instant messaging and social networks. However, this should by no means be taken to indicate that e-mail itself is in decline. Indeed, to quote further statistics from Radicati, the 1.4 billion e-mail users of 2009 are set to rise to 1.9 billion by 2013, with worldwide traffic increasing from 247 billion messages per day to 507 billion in the same period.[2]

Given the importance of the medium, it is no surprise that e-mail security is now an extremely significant issue. Indeed, a 2007 report from the European Network and Information Security Agency (ENISA) revealed that 'email and electronic communications' was considered to be the most important area in which organisations should ensure staff awareness of security topics or risks.[3] The fact that this placed it ahead of a whole range of other key issues (including physical security, passwords, Internet security and viruses) helps to illustrate just how significant the use of email has now become. Later chapters consequently focus upon the ways in which both messages and services ought to be protected. To begin with, however, attention is turned to the risks that such reliance upon e-mail can pose in its own right.

Dependency without a guarantee

The reliance upon e-mail has become so engrained within many businesses that things can no longer function nearly as well without it. Indeed, in extreme situations, there are some people that are so dependent upon e-mail that they literally don't know what to do if the system is down, and find that many of their daily tasks are oriented around their e-mail. Whether this is a good thing is clearly open to question, especially given that e-mail itself is not a completely reliable medium in the first place. Indeed, while most senders will work on the assumption that once they have successfully sent an e-mail it will also be successfully received at the other end, the reality is that there are several circumstances in which

---

[2] Radicati. 2009. 'The Radicati Group Releases "Email Statistics Report, 2009–2013"', Press Release, Radicati Group Inc., 6 May 2009.
[3] ENISA. 2007. *Information security awareness initiatives: Current practice and the measurement of success.* European Network and Information Security Agency, July 2007.

messages may not actually reach the recipient as intended. One of the most common is that they get misclassified as spam (junk) mail, and either get blocked at the recipient's mail server or placed into a junk folder on their local machine rather than going into the inbox as normal. As a result, the message may only be spotted some time later (e.g. if the recipient does a periodic trawl of their junk folder to check the messages) or may go unnoticed altogether (e.g. if the recipient is the sort of person who just purges their junk mail without looking at it).

The underlying cause of the difficulty here is, of course, the problem posed by *genuine* spam mail. This has now become so significant that simply letting it all through would represent a significant overhead, in terms of both the technical demands (e.g. wasted bandwidth and storage) and human effort (e.g. wasting time having to sift through all the junk in order to find the messages that actually matter). As a result, many e-mail systems have evolved to incorporate spam-filtering techniques, which try to reduce the burden by looking for signs of spam messages and then flagging and/or separating out those that look suspicious. However, the classification process is far from perfect, and from the authors' personal experience it is not unusual to find one or two legitimate emails per day that have been misclassified as spam, and which, therefore, end up in the junk folder rather than the inbox (plus, of course, occasional spam messages that still manage to make it through). To illustrate the point, the header of a related example is shown in Figure 1. The reasons are not always predictable, but common causes include e-mails that do not have a substantial message body (e.g. those that only include a hyperlink or an attachment) or messages that have been sent to multiple recipients. Somewhat ironically then, spam filtering can effectively become a threat to the overall integrity of operations if the errors are not identified and messages get missed as a result.

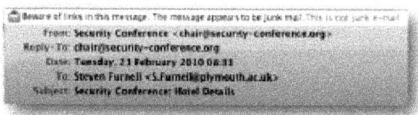

Figure 1: A legitimate message, but misclassified as spam and filed as junk mail

Unfortunately, being mistakenly treated as spam is just one of the reasons that things may not go to plan. Other options that may lead to messaging failure include:

- routing problems within the network, with the consequence that the process times out and the message never actually finds a path to the intended destination;

- messages arriving only to find that the recipient's mailbox is full and, therefore, cannot accommodate them;

- blocking of particular message types at the remote end or stripping of attachments, meaning that recipients do not get to see the content that was intended.

In some cases the sender may get a message back to advise them of a problem, but even then the timeliness of such notifications may vary. For example, whereas a full mailbox is likely to yield a fairly immediate auto-reply, delay notifications may not appear until hours (or even days) after the original despatch of the message. In the event of their message being misclassified as spam, it is unlikely that the sender would receive any indication, and so recovering the situation largely rests with whether or not the recipient checks their junk mail and/or whether the sender tries to follow it up later.

The implications of dependence

To answer the question posed by the chapter title, the likely response from many would now be 'not very easily'. It's easy to become blase about our adoption and reliance upon e-mail, because its use is already so engrained that it seems obvious. However, what is less certain is whether we have fully recognised the implications. In fact, whether we are new or established users, the prevalence of e-mail ought to raise some important questions from a security perspective:

- What risks does it introduce?

- Do people know how to use it effectively?

- Do they know how to use it safely?

• What safeguards can technology provide?

The answers to these and other issues are addressed as part of the chapters that follow.

Takeaways

➤ Recognise the level of dependency that your organisation has upon e-mail relative to other forms of communication, and ensure that security issues are afforded appropriate priority accordingly.

➤ Do not allow the speed and convenience of email to compromise the credibility of business decisions. If an issue requires proper debate, a rapid but ill-considered e-mail reply may pose as much of a threat as a deliberate attack.

➤ Do not assume that e-mail recipients are guaranteed to receive the messages you intend for them. Although it works most of the time, you cannot be sure that a message has got through until you get a reply or do something to check.

➤ Recognise that different users may prioritise and handle e-mails in different ways. If something requires urgent action or explicit confirmation then consider that alternative channels may need to be used.

➤ Ensure that users are aware of the organisation's expectations regarding e-mail usage and frequency of checking (e.g. if they are expected to keep a watchful eye on messages, then they need to be advised that checking once or twice per day is not sufficient).

➤ Perform periodic checks of junk mail folders to ensure that relevant and important messages have not found their way there by mistake. Once checked, folders can be purged to keep their size down.

CHAPTER 2: E-MAIL THREATS AND ATTACKS

Alongside the undoubted benefits, a variety of risks can be introduced via e-mail channels, affecting individuals, systems and organisations. This chapter considers problems originating from the messages themselves, such as spam and phishing, as well as the potential for messages to become carriers for malware such as viruses, worms and Trojan horses. The discussion highlights the threat vectors, illustrating them with appropriate examples, alongside advice for reducing the associated risk and disruption.

E-mail can undoubtedly offer us an easy and effective means of communication. Unfortunately, it also represents a significant channel for threats to both organisations and individuals. Indeed, many of these are well established and organisations have already been forced into providing safeguards against the problems. For example, 97% of businesses surveyed in the UK's *2008 Information Security Breaches Survey* (ISBS) filtered incoming e-mail for spam and 95% scanned it for malware.[4] In addition, there are further isssues that can arise from within the organisation. For instance, of the 16% of ISBS respondents reporting staff misuse of information systems, almost half (7%) were related to e-mail access. Moreover, when considering only the large organisations (rather than the respondent base as a whole) the proportion experiencing e-mail misuse rose to a quarter. In terms of the volume of associated incidents, approximately half of the affected respondents were reporting only 'a few' during the prior year. However, at the extreme end of the scale, almost one in ten were reporting several misuse incidents per day.

The focus of this chapter is primarily placed upon the threats that may enter the organisation via email, with the problems

---

[4] BERR. 2008. *2008 Information Security Breaches Survey – Technical Report.* Department for Business Enterprise & Regulatory Reform, April 2008. URN 08/788.

arising from staff misuse being more fully pursued in Chapter 8. With this in mind, a good starting point is the significant threat posed by e-mail-based malicious code ...

Mass-mailed malware

Although Internet-wide incidents had been experienced before (e.g. the Internet Worm, or Morris Worm, of 1988 was able to infect the entire network via a combination of vulnerability exploits), the mass adoption of e-mail was a catalyst for ushering in truly large-scale and more frequent malware incidents. Landmark cases such as the Melissa virus and the Love Letter worm were fundamentally possible because they used email as their distribution channel. While later years have seen fewer celebrity cases of this nature, the problem has far from disappeared. To illustrate the point, Figure 2 draws upon data from MessageLabs and depicts the changing picture over the past decade, with the worst period having been in 2004, with an average of one in every sixteen messages being infected.

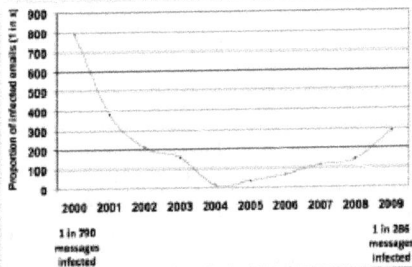

Figure 2: Proportion of malware-infected e-mail from 2000 to 2009

As a consequence of the threat, e-mail protection is now a standard feature of antivirus and Internet security packages, and e-mail clients themselves now incorporate features to block potentially suspicious attachments and executable scripts. However, this is one of the many areas of security in which technology alone cannot provide the complete solution. Many malware-related e-mails (and indeed wider e-mail scams that are discussed later in the chapter) seek to exploit people via social engineering. For example, the aforementioned Melissa virus claimed to be an important message containing a document requested by the recipient,[5] whereas (as its name suggests) the Love Letter worm found success by claiming that its attachment was a love letter.[6] In fact, the methods and guises that malware may employ are so variable that it is difficult to provide specific advice to staff beyond exercising caution with attachments and any messages that do not contain expected work-related content.

Organisations appear to be fairly well attuned to the need to protect themselves against incoming problems, with the aforementioned 2008 ISBS reporting that 95% scanned incoming e-mail and web downloads for malware. However, there appears to be somewhat less recognition of the importance of scanning *outgoing* mail, with only 77% claiming to do so. As such, malware that may have entered the organisation via another route (e.g. on removable media or an infected laptop) may then find an unprotected channel for spreading onwards and outwards to other systems.

In fact, scans of outgoing e-mails can also be utilised to safeguard against a variety of other threats relating to content that employees should not be sending. However, as Figure 3 illustrates, only a minority of organisations tend to scan for things other than malware (with the identification of inappropriate content being the next most likely target, but still trailing by a considerable margin). The finding that a fifth of organisations scan for nothing at all clearly goes some way to explaining why other organisations still face a considerable volume of incoming threats.

---

[5] CERT. 1999. 'CERT® Advisory CA-1999-04 Melissa Macro Virus', 27 March 1999.
www.cert.org/advisories/CA-1999-04.html
[6] CERT. 2000. 'CERT® Advisory CA-2000-04 Love Letter Worm', 4 May 2000.
www.cert.org/advisories/CA-2000-04.html

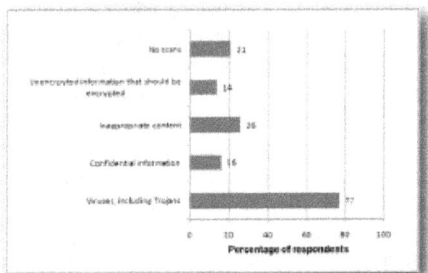

Figure 3: Things scanned for in outgoing e-mails (Source: BERR 2008 ISBS)

Technical countermeasures for handling malware (plus the other threats mentioned here) are discussed in later chapters.

Spams and scams

While e-mail has undoubtedly been a boon to both business and personal communications, it has also provided an easy route for the considerable volume of unwanted messages that now reach us. While junk mail existed in pre-e-mail days, the provision of the electronic channel means that it can now address a vast audience, and it can do so quickly, in high volumes and at minimal cost. Indeed, the sheer ease of sending messages has amplified the junk mail problem out of all recognition, with the knock-on consequence that virtually all e-mail users are familiar with the nuisance posed by spam. Consequently, as mentioned in Chapter 1, spam-filtering technologies are now a standard element of e-mail *13* provision, and it has been estimated that managing the problem costs upwards of US$1.8 million per annum for a typical 1,000-user organisation.[7] As an aside, spam is also an issue to be aware of in relation to messages being *sent,* in order to ensure that we are not contributing to the problem. This is especially relevant in view of increasing anti-spam legislation

---

[7] Radicati. 2009. 'The Radicati Group Releases "Email Statistics Report, 2009-2013"', Press Release, Radicati Group Inc., 6 May 2009.

(e.g. the US CAN-SPAM Act[8]), which can hold organisations accountable for sending spam and levy fines if they misbehave.

The nature of the unwanted messages that we can receive in this manner is variable. While many still fit into the mould of advertising-related junk mail that can still be regularly received by post, they are accompanied by more insidious messages that seek to dupe and defraud the recipients. A common example here is the so-called advance fee fraud (also referred to as 419 scams after the related article of the Nigerian criminal code) in which recipients are promised a large sum of money in return for assisting with a financial transaction. The example in Figure 4 is typical of the genre, with a combined appeal to the trust and greed of the recipient (combined in this case with the potential added incentive of becoming the guardian of a 20-year-old woman). Within the rather lengthy body of the message, a notable aspect is the mention of 'Tax you will pay during the transfer'. This is basically an indication of the ensuing sting, when anyone responding to the message and expressing interest will find that there are various up-front fees to be paid before any money can actually be transferred to their account. And, of course, the reality is that, if things were allowed to proceed, this would be the *only* money that would ever actually change hands.

From: Miss.Lucy Naumi

Country: Cote d'Ivoire

DEAR FRIEND

My Dear, I saw your contact through the Internet directory and after going through your profile my instinct advised me to contact you, while I was searching for someone who can assist me in this great time of need, someone who can

---

[8] FTC. 2009. 'The CAN-SPAM Act: A Compliance Guide for Business', Federal Trade Commission, September 2009. *www.ftc.gov/bcp/edu/pubs/business/ecommerce/bus61.shtm* (accessed 1 September 2010).

help me out of this my present predicament.Please, carefully read below to understand my plight. I need someone, whom I can trust and someone who would be also sincere to me. I am writing to you hoping that you would accord and give me the needed help and assistance that I am looking for.

My name is Lucy Naumi, I'm the only Child/daughter of late mr. and mrs. Macoli Naumi. My father was a very Wealthy Timber & African art Merchant, the Chairman board of trustee, of all farm products exporters. (C.F.E) here in Abidjan the Economic Capital of Cote d'Ivoire6, before the death of my father on 28th August 2009. He was poison by his business associate due to he was a successful man and had a lot of money and property.

He made it clear to me that he deposited the sum of ($9.5, 000, 000, 00 US DOLLARS)

NINE MILLION FIVE HUNDRED THOUSAND UNITED STATE AMERICAN DOLLARS. Was deposited in fixed deposit account in my name as the next of kin in a SECURITY FINANCE COMPANY, here in Abidjan, Cote d'Ivoire. Because he new that his people will not let me lay my hand on any of his properties that is why he deposited that money in a fixed account for me to have access to it only. With a Clause that, In his demise. As only member of the family, I can have access to the funds only if im 28 or i should look for a foreign partner who will assist me to invest the Funds abroad

Dear, I have all the relevant documents my late father used in depositing the money in the Bank right now with me and I can forward them to you on your demand for your view as soon as i hear from you and confirm you're truly to assist me.

I am humbly seeking for your assistance in these following ways:

---

1. To provide a Bank account where the money will be transferred into for investment purpose.

2. To serve as my guardian because I am a girl of 20 years old.

3. To find a good university in your country where I can further my education.

I am willing to offer you 15% of the total sum as compensation for your effort input and mapped out 5% for any Tax you will pay during the transfer. Furthermore, if you indicate your opinion towards this matter as I will like us to conclude this transaction within (14) working days, if you are with me endeavour to make it known soonest. Because I am presently in a Hotel here in Abidjan for the safety of my life.

Thanks and may God bless you.

You can contact me through my private e-mail lucynaumi@yahoo.cn

With Love,

Miss. Lucy Naumi

Figure 4: An indicative example of a '419' advance fee fraud

Despite the fact that they are badly written and implausible, scams, such as that in Figure 4, are still in circulation today and clearly still have the potential to snare sufficient victims for the efforts to be worthwhile. Indeed, the fact that e-mail enables the scammers to cast such a wide net means that most of the potential victims do not *need* to fall for it. The economics are such that it still pays off if only a tiny percentage of naive and greedy recipients actually take the bait. On the positive side, many such messages now get automatically classified as spam, thus helping to warn potentially susceptible recipients about their questionable provenance.

There's something phishy going on

Staying with the theme of fraudulent messages, we come to the specific category of phishing, so named because perpetrators use the messages to fish for sensitive information from any recipients that they manage to hook. The aim is to trick the user with an e-mail that purports to come from a legitimate source and which presents some pretext for requiring information from them (typically collected via an accompanying website). A good definition of the general problem is provided by the Anti-Phishing Working Group (APWG):

a criminal mechanism employing both *social* engineering and *technical subterfuge* to steal consumers' personal identity data and financial account credentials[9]

Phishing represents a significant threat, with the APWG receiving an average of 30,880 unique phishing message reports per month in the last quarter of 2009, alongside an average of 45,873 unique phishing websites being detected per month in the same period. As an example of the problem, a typical message is presented in Figure 5. In this case the message is not particularly convincing, with rather untidy formatting and a solicitation to follow a link that does not look remotely like it belongs to the bank HSBC (the claimed sender). However, there is still a risk that a naive HSBC customer might receive it and be so concerned by the potential for their account to be disrupted that they comply with the request without thinking.

---

[9] APWG. 2010. *Phishing Activity Trends Report – 4th Quarter 2009.* October –December 2009. Anti-Phishing Working Group. *www.apwg.org/reports/apwg%20report%20Q4%202009.pdf* (accessed 1 September 2010).

Dear valued HSBC® member:

Due to concerns, for the safety and integrity of the HSBC internet banking services we have issued this warning message.

However, failure to update your records will result in delays in services rendered. Please update your records on or before March 08th, 2010.

Once you have updated your internet banking record your HSBC account service will not be interrupted and will continue as normal.

To update your HSBC® records click on the following link.

Click here to updated your account <http://brx.htbe.ru/new.htm>

Thank You.
HSBC® UPDATE TEAM

Accounts Management As outlined in our User Agreement, HSBC® will periodically send you information about site changes and enhancements.

Visit our Privacy Policy and User Agreement if you have any questions http://www.hsbc.co.uk ® 2010

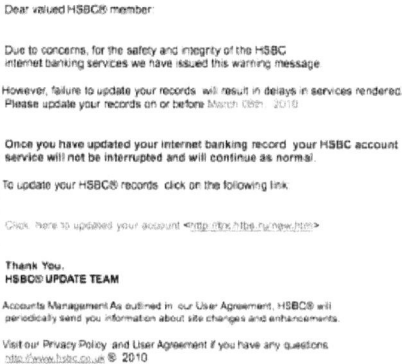

Figure 5: An example of a phishing message

The targeting of HSBC in this example demonstrates the wider problem facing online brands, which may find their name being used as the basis for a scam and their customers being targeted as the intended victims. According to the 2008 ISBS,[10] companies across every sector reported phishing incidents in which their brand had been impersonated by e-mail. In most cases, this was fairly infrequent, with 50% reporting one incident and 31% reporting 'a few'. However, among the remainder there was somewhat more of a problem, with 9% of respondents experiencing one incident per month, a further 9% one per week and 1% claiming daily occurrence. The findings also reported that companies accepting online orders were slightly more likely to find themselves being targeted.

One of the challenges of handling phishing is that there is no definitive checklist of visible indicators that you can use to ensure that a message is genuine. There are certainly some things that you might look out for in order to raise suspicion (e.g. messages claiming to be from credible sources that appear

---

[10] BERR. 2008. *2008 Information Security Breaches Survey – Technical Report.* Department for Business Enterprise & Regulatory Reform, April 2008. URN 08/788.

unprofessionally formatted or poorly written, that seek to guide you to an address that does not appear to match the claimed source, or which ask you to verify account details), but the key point is that the absence of such indicators still does not mean that a message is actually safe.

The fundamental point is that it is very difficult to judge the legitimacy of a message from appearances alone. Indeed, to illustrate the point we can consider the findings from a study in which 179 end-users were asked to consider 20 potential phishing messages, and determine whether they thought each was legitimate or not.[11] The messages covered a variety of online scenarios including banking, retailers and auction services; in reality, 11 of the messages were phishing attempts, while the remainder were legitimate. However, as can be seen in Table 1, the level of successful classification by the participants was hardly impressive and would seem to be no better than one might expect from potluck.

	Correctly classified	Incorrectly classified	Don't know
Legitimate messages	36%	37%	27%
Illegitimate messages	45.5%	28.5%	26%
Overall	42%	32%	26%

Table 1: End-user attempts to classify phishing messages by appearance alone

A key factor here was that the messages were removed from any surrounding context (e.g. a user receiving a message from an online bank that they did not bank with would have an immediate basis for suspicion), and the participants were unable to perform checks such as looking at the destination of hyperlinks, viewing message headers or examining the

---

[11] Furnell, S. 2007. 'Phishing: can we spot the signs?', *Computer Fraud & Security,* March 2007, pp10-15.

HyperText Markup Language (HTML). The results did, however, serve to prove that phishing messages do not necessarily stand out quite as prominently as some users may otherwise expect.

Another notable point from an organisation's perspective is that some phishing scams are more specifically targeted, and may aim to acquire information that primarily compromises the business rather than the individual. The specific term for this is *spear phishing,* and at this point, the concept departs somewhat from the aforementioned APWG definition because the victims are not necessarily consumers, and the target data tends to relate more towards login and access credentials, or company confidential information, rather than personal and financial details.

One of the reasons that spear phishing works is because the phisher is able to demonstrate a more specific knowledge of the recipient and/or their organisation, and, therefore, present a more plausible and convincing pretext. It is, therefore, important for users to be made aware that the phishing threat is not limited to the generic 'validate your bank account details' messages that they may be used to seeing.

Takeaways

➤ Ensure the scanning of both incoming *and* outgoing e-mails for malware.

➤ Be aware of the risks posed by particular forms of e-mail attachments (e.g. scripts and executables, and archive/compressed files within which they may be hidden).

➤ Raise staff awareness of phishing threats, with particular attention given to spear-phishing approaches that might be used to target them as employees of the organisation. Particular emphasis should be given to the fact that phishing messages may not stand out as obviously as some people may expect.

> ➤ When receiving an e-mail that asks you to do something or provide some information, give careful consideration to how reasonable it is and whether you can check its provenance. Consider the scope for misusing any information you may divulge and whether the request can/should be referred to someone else.

> ➤ If your brand is likely to be hijacked by scams such as phishing, be sure to offer related guidance to your clients via other channels (e.g. on your website).

CHAPTER 3: SECURING THE CLIENT

There is a wide range of potential e-mail clients available to organisational users, with each offering a potentially bewildering range of security options. This chapter considers the related features commonly integrated within mail clients (including WebMail systems), together with other issues that may need to be considered as part of an organisation's policies and procedures.

One issue facing many organisations is the perception that security is taken care of centrally by the system administrators rather than it being a shared responsibility facing all employees. There are obviously many ways to implement security for e-mail systems and inevitably much of this will be done at the server end. However, modern email clients also offer comprehensive facilities for improving security, and it is relevant to consider and use these capabilities.

General guidelines

Most mail clients offer user-configurable settings (or some mechanism to deploy an organisation-wide policy) that affect how the client behaves in certain contexts. While by no means providing a definitive list, this section provides some general pointers to what should be considered best practice (or even minimum standards) in relation to these features.

Anti-virus/phishing/spam: Most clients will support some level of integration with commercial anti-virus tools. This is often coupled with automatic scanning of incoming e-mails for indicators of phishing/spam content. Messages flagged as suspicious or containing spam/phishing indicators are often moved to quarantine folders where users have the option to review the filtering decisions or restore blocked e-mails. Users need to be aware that these mechanisms are not 100% reliable and there will always be a proportion of false positives (messages incorrectly classified as malicious/suspicious) and false negatives (messages overlooked and still presented in the user's inbox).

Attachments: Even when messages are checked by anti-virus scanning, users should still exercise caution when opening *any* attachments, even when the message appears to be from a trusted individual. Attachments can easily contain malware that is unknown to the user's anti-virus product, which could then run potentially unchallenged. It is also possible that e-mail attachments could be encrypted with a password provided in the body of the message (with encrypted attachments not accessible to anti-virus products). Even compressed archives (e.g. ZIP) may be used to hide malware (although most anti-virus products are able to open common compression file formats). Users should also be aware of double file extensions (where the real extension is hidden by the mail client – e.g. holiday.jpg.exe, which may appear as the sender's latest holiday photos but actually contains an executable file).

Attachment blocking: Most mail clients support attachment blocking (with some enabled by default), generally preventing executable file attachments (including .exe, .com, .bat, .pif, etc. and often script files, e.g. .js, .vbs, .asp, etc.) from being opened. While this is useful for the majority of users, organisations should be aware that this may be limiting in some cases (e.g. a website developer sending a script file to a colleague). Organisations may wish to develop policies relating to acceptable e-mail file types (both for sending and receiving).

Attachment size: Although not an immediately obvious security issue, many organisations limit the maximum attachment size. This is usually done to prevent exceptionally large files from filling mailboxes (and reducing processing, bandwidth and ultimately cost). However, it may be desirable to limit attachment sizes to restrict information leakage (preventing employees from exporting large volumes of data via e-mail).

Encryption: There are two main options for providing encryption facilities in most e-mail clients (including some WebMail clients):

1   Pretty Good Privacy (PGP), which was developed by Phil
    Zimmermann in 1991 and provides asymmetric encryption
    (and signing) of messages. PGP (and more recently
    OpenPGP/GPG – Gnu Privacy Guard) is commonly used
    for personal users rather than organisations (which often
    prefer S/MIME (Secure/Multipurpose Internet Mail
    Extensions) due to the integration with existing User
    Agents (UAs)/servers). PGP uses a public/private key pair
    that allows the public key of a recipient to be widely
    distributed (even by unencrypted e-mail) – effectively
    removing the classic key distribution problem. However, it
    is heavily dependent on *trust* and a requirement to
    distribute the necessary keys to all recipients prior to secure
    communication. In receiving a public key via an insecure
    medium, the recipient has to determine if the key is from a
    trusted source – this can be addressed through the use of
    signed keys where a chain of trust is developed through
    friends of friends. Essentially, the security that PGP offers
    is intrinsically linked to the secrecy of the private key and
    the trusted network of friends who validate the legitimacy
    of new public keys.

2   S/MIME operates in a similar manner to PGP, except that
    instead of using keys (with a requirement to self-
    distribute), it utilises a hierarchy of digitally signed
    certificates. For example, an organisation may purchase a
    suitable certificate with which it may digitally sign
    personal certificates for each employee. These certificates
    can then be integrated into many mail server platforms (e.g.
    Exchange Global Address List) to allow transparent
    encryption and message signing for internal users (with
    most mail clients offering integrated support for S/MIME –
    a distinct advantage over PGP). Sending encrypted content
    to an external user requires possession of their public key;
    this can be easily provided through an exchange of digitally
    signed emails. Providing an e-mail recipient is able to
    verify the legitimacy of the original certifying authority
    (usually automatic), there is an implicit trust of the
    individual users. Figure 6 shows how a user can verify an
    encrypted email in Microsoft® Office Outlook® and Mail
    under OSX.

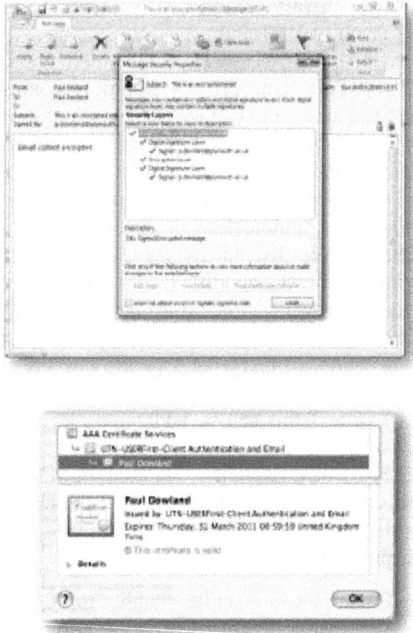

**Figure 6: Verification of an encrypted e-mail in Microsoft®
Office Outlook® (top) and Mail under OSX (bottom)**

Digitally signed e-mail: Using S/MIME or PGP it is possible
to sign an e-mail, which provides the recipient with a visual
confirmation of the sender and that the message content has not
been modified (Figure 7 illustrates this point by showing both
signed and encrypted e-mails in Microsoft® Office Outlook®).
S/MIME also allows for easy revocation of digital certificates
through the certificating authority. Many certificate providers
offer free trials that allow users to investigate the use of signed
(and/or encrypted) email.

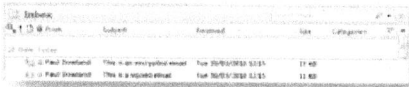

**Figure 7: Signed and encrypted e-mails in Microsoft®
Office Outlook® 2007**

HTML e-mail: Again, this is not an obvious security threat,
but, HTML-based e-mails may contain embedded code (e.g.
VBScript, JavaScript), iframes (downloading content from
external websites) or other objects (e.g. Java applets, ActiveX
objects, media components) that may be acting as a Trojan
horse for malware. Most clients are also able to suppress
images that may contain inappropriate content or that can
provide a web-bug (a graphical image hosted on a web server
that is used to confirm the legitimacy of an e-mail address by
logging a uniquely coded Uniform Resource Locator (URL)
request). The options for restricting images (and some other
HTML content) embedded in e-mails within Microsoft® Office
Outlook® are illustrated in Figure 8.

**Figure 8: Trust centre options in Microsoft® Office
Outlook® 2007 for HTML e-mails**

Hyperlinks: E-mails often contain hyperlinks and, in most
cases, are linked directly to the appropriate website.
Unfortunately, when using HTML e-mail, it is easy to provide
a textual link (possibly showing a URL) that then links to a
completely different site. Users should be familiar with the
risks of following hyperlinks and should also be in the habit of
reporting suspicious URLs, as these could be blocked by the
organisation's firewall if considered a rissk to other users.

Recalling e-mail: This feature is not provided by any of the underlying protocols. Instead, this is a facility in Microsoft e-mail clients/servers to allow users to recall messages that have been sent inadvertently or incorrectly. This is not a reliable mechanism, since a recalled message may have already been read, transferred to another system or forwarded, or the recipient may be using a non-Microsoft client that does not provide message-recalling services. There may also be concerns over the use of message recalling, as a user acting on instructions contained in an e-mail may have no 'evidence' if the original sender subsequently recalls the message (or a third party spoofs a message recall).

Sensitivity classification (normal/confidential): This is another Microsoft feature that allows users to attribute a confidentiality flag to individual emails. Classifications available include 'personal', 'private' and 'confidential'. It is important to note that these classifications do not imply any form of protection (e.g. encryption) – they are simple flags that are interpreted by Microsoft mail clients to visually indicate an implied level of confidentiality.

Web-based clients

Web-based clients typically offer a limited subset of the functionality of their desktop counterparts. However, this difference is becoming less significant as the trend to a mobile workforce has influenced the development of more advanced WebMail features. Figure 9 shows the junk e-mail filtering facilities integrated into Microsoft® Office Outlook® Web Access (OWA), which provides a WebMail interface to the Microsoft® Exchange mail server. These options effectively replicate the same functionality that would be available in a typical desktop client (providing white lists for senders – *Safe Senders)* together with a blacklist for blocked senders (by e-mail address or domain). In this example it is also possible to include a safe recipient list to accept e-mails for a number of addresses (e.g. to handle redirected e-mail).

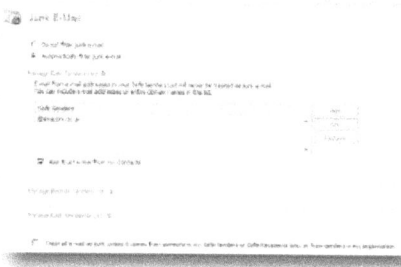

Figure 9: Junk mail filtering in Microsoft® Office Outlook® Web Access (OWA)

Mobile clients

With the increasingly mobile workforce, many employees now synchronise mobile phones/Personal Digital Assistants (PDAs) to the organisational e-mail servers (sometimes without permission) with the consequent risks from device theft and loss. Fortunately, some mail servers offer the ability to remotely wipe a lost or stolen device (see Figure 10), but it should be considered that the ability to remotely wipe a device may be limited, especially if the new *owner* doesn't connect the device to the Internet before trying to access the locally stored data.

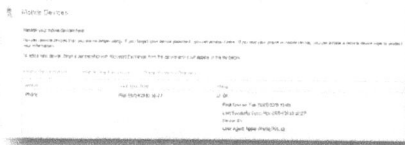

Figure 10: Mobile device management in Microsoft® Exchange

In addition to the local synchronisation of phones/PDAs (typically by Universal Serial Bus (USB)), users are likely to increasingly use WLAN/3G (3rd Generation) connections to connect to mail services. Although most of these devices will support secure protocols (OWA over Secure Sockets Layer

(SSL), POP3/IMAP over SSL, etc.), it is possible for them to be configured to use protocols that do not encrypt credentials (or the e-mail content). Consideration should be given to policies relating to the use of mobile devices – especially to the use of personal devices. In addition, administrators should be aware of the changing legal landscape (taking, for example, the recent demands in India, Saudi Arabia and the United Arab Emirates for government access to data transported via the BlackBerry service[12]).

Takeaways

➢ Have a clear policy on the use of attachments covering (both in terms of sending and receiving):

   ➢ appropriateness of content

   ➢ attachment size

   ➢ attachment type

   ➢ export of corporate data.

➢ Ensure users have a clear understanding of email client features and an appreciation of the security implications (e.g. an e-mail flagged as confidential receives no more protection than any other).

➢ Consider the use of encryption for sensitive email correspondence. Users will need to be made aware of the facility and what they are required to do in order to use it.

➢ Have a clear policy on synchronisation of corporate e-mail with personal devices, together with a mechanism to remotely wipe lost and stolen devices.

---

[12] BBC. 2010. 'India sets Blackberry monitoring deadline', BBC News Online, 17 August 2010. *www.bbc.co.uk/news/technology-10998549* (accessed 1 September 2010)

CHAPTER 4: SAFETY IN TRANSIT

This chapter considers the threats to e-mail while travelling across networks and between devices, e.g. through corporate networks, home networks, mail relays and Internet Service Providers (ISPs). Consideration is given to the potential for interception/modification of e-mail along the journey and the various mechanisms for protecting e-mail outside of the control of an organisation.

The previous chapter identified a range of protective mechanisms for e-mail on the client-side. However, once e-mail has left the user's desktop, there are a myriad of risks that an e-mail can face while *in transit*. These risks relate back to the fundamental principles of security, notably:

* confidentiality: ensuring that the e-mail content is not disclosed to a third party;

* integrity: ensuring that the e-mail's content cannot be modified before reaching its destination;

* availability: ensuring that the mail servers (including any additional mail relays *en route)* are not adversely affected (e.g. by denial of service attacks);

* authenticity: ensuring that the sender (and recipient) are the genuine parties concerned;

* non-repudiation: proving that the claimed sender did indeed send the message.

Before considering the risks and the possible countermeasures, it is perhaps useful to consider briefly the different network protocols used for email communication.

Protocols

Once e-mail has left an organisation (and often even internally), the most common protocol for forwarding e-mails is the Simple Mail Transfer Protocol (SMTP). SMTP is a plain text protocol that operates over Transmission Control Protocol (TCP) port 25. [13] [14] The plain text nature allows for easy observation of the header and content of emails in transit – hence without further protection e-mail confidentiality cannot be guaranteed. To illustrate this point, Figure 11 shows an example session between a client and a server via SMTP.

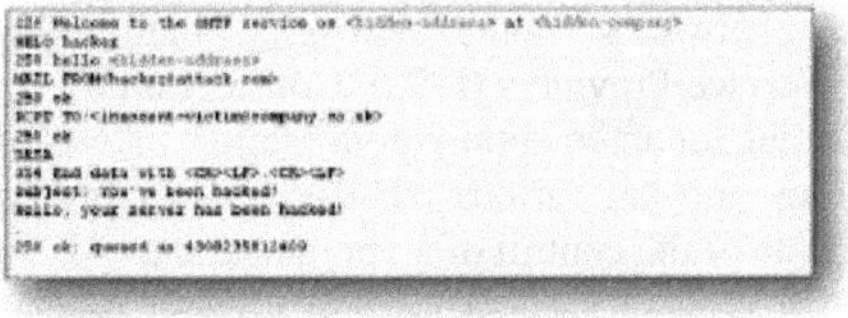

Figure 11: An example SMTP communication session

The traffic in the figure was acquired using Wireshark, an open source, freely available packet-capturing tool. Using Wireshark (or even command prompt tools such as tcpdump/windump), it is possible to capture live network traffic and filter for specific protocols (e.g. SMTP). This captured traffic can easily be saved for later analysis.

Although there are SMTP variations that allow for encrypted credentials (for authenticated relaying) and encrypted mail transfer (e.g. using SSL/TLS (Transport Layer Security)), as most e-mail ultimately leaves organisational boundaries, it is impractical to require authentication or encryption for Internet-bound e-mail forwarding. This ultimately provides multiple 'monitoring' locations in which a third party can potentially log on and view the contents of the messages (within the organisation, throughout the ISPs through which the traffic is transmitted and at the destination).

Although it is unlikely that there will be universal acceptance of secure versions of SMTP (SSL/TLS), these should still be

---

[13] RFC 821 'Simple Mail Transfer Protocol', 1982, Internet Engineering Task Force (IETF). *http://tools.ietf.org/html/rfc821* (accessed 1 September 2010)
[14] RFC 5321 'Simple Mail Transfer Protocol', 2008, IETF. *http://tools.ietf.org/html/rfc5321* (accessed 1 September 2010)

considered the preferred approach – especially internally, where the use of SMTP should be considered as a last resort.

SMTP is used exclusively for forwarding of e-mail messages to their final destination server, at which point the e-mail will normally wait in the appropriate user' s mailbox. Although there are a number of standardised mechanisms for retrieving e-mail from the local server, traditionally this has used the Post Office Protocol (POP). [15] This is again a plain text protocol, but, unlike SMTP, POP always requires user credentials to identify and authenticate the legitimate user for the requested mailbox. Unfortunately, this places such credentials in the hands of a protocol, which (in its native form) offers no direct protection. Figure 12 shows another example where a simple network-monitoring tool can access the message content of an e-mail during delivery (while also capturing the user credentials of the recipient).

Figure 12: An example POP3 session showing plain text authentication and message content

Although the original implementation of POP utilised plain text authentication, later versions have introduced enhanced security. For example, authenticated POP (APOP) (defined in POP3) uses the Message-Digest algorithm 5 (MD5) to conceal the user's password (unfortunately, due to increasingly cheap

---

[15] RFC 1939 'Post Office Protocol – Version 3', 1996, IETF. *http://tools.ietf.org/html/rfc1939* (accessed 1 September 2010)

computer power, this is now vulnerable to brute force or rainbow table-based attacks[16]).

The Internet Message Access Protocol (IMAP) [17] offers an alternative to POP for remote mailbox access. IMAP offers extensive mailbox functions (beyond those offered by POP), as well as supporting SSL/TLS encryption to protect authentication credentials. Although IMAP should be considered the preferred option for accessing mailboxes, not all clients or servers support this protocol. Some consideration also needs to be given to the sending of e-mail (which is still likely to need SMTP).

It should be noted that the weaknesses identified in these protocols are not negated by only using them within organisational boundaries, as internal users could just as easily utilise packet-capturing techniques to steal data and credentials.

WebMail users (and many mobile users) will use entirely different protocols, but only for communication between their device (running a web browser/mail client) and the server. Exchanges between client and server typically run over HyperText Transfer Protocol Secure (HTTPS), which offers a high level of security. However, users need to be aware of the importance of certificates and understand browser (or client) warnings that may indicate a man-in-the-middle[18] (or man-in-the-browser[19]) attack (Figure 13).

---

[16] 16 md5(); website, 2008. *http://md5.rednoize.com/* (accessed 1 September 2010)

[17] RFC 3501 ''Internet Message Access Protocol – Version 4rev1'', 2003, IETF. *http://tools.ietf.org/html/rfc3501* (accessed 1 September 2010)

[18] 'Open Web Application Security Project (OWASP) 'Man-in-the-middle attack', 2009 *www.owasp.org/index.php/Man-in-the-middle_attack* (accessed 1 September 2010)

[19] Gühring, P., 'Concepts against Man-in-the-Browser Attacks', 2006. *www2.futureware.at/svn/sourcerer/CAcert/SecureClient.pdf* (accessed 1 September 2010)

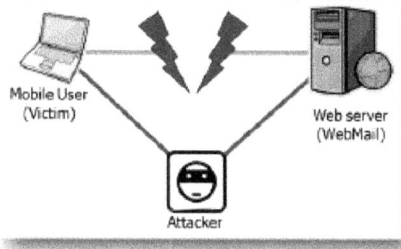

Figure 13: Man-in-the-middle attack

The screenshots in Figure 14 show examples of browser certificate warnings (taken from Mozilla® Firefox® and Microsoft® Internet Explorer® respectively – additional examples based upon other popular browsers can be found in the Appendix). Although the inclusion of these warnings alerts users to the possible problems with a server certificate, many users will not understand what the error message actually means. Users should, therefore, be made familiar with typical warning messages and be provided with appropriate training to understand the warning, evaluate the risk and make an informed judgement.

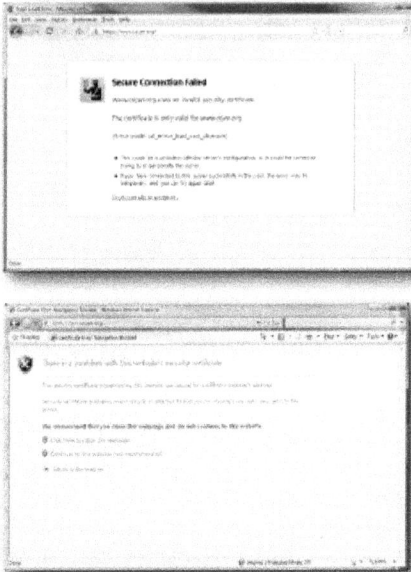

**Figure 14: Example security certificate warnings in
Mozilla® Firefox® v3 (top) and Microsoft® Internet
Explorer® 8 (bottom)**

It should be noted that running WebMail (or another client) via
HTTP will render all traffic vulnerable to the same
compromises as SMTP or POP, as this is also an unencrypted
protocol. Although the viewing and generation of e-mails is
likely to be secure between client and server, emails leaving
the protection of the organisation's network (destined to
external servers) are likely to be sent via standard SMTP, with
users potentially unaware of the security implications once
messages leave the presumed secure website.

Countermeasures

Although many of the issues described in this chapter can be
addressed by the use of authentication and/or encryption, this
will generally only provide protection within an organisation's

own network. The main reason for this is that it is not feasible to expect or require a remote mail system to comply with a set of security criteria specific to your organisation. Each individual mail server is likely to handle thousands of connections from a variety of sources, each potentially capable of supporting a range of countermeasures – with many unable to offer more than simple SMTP. Unless the communication is pre-arranged (for example, between remote sites of a single organisation where an SSL/TLS connection may be established), it is likely that all external e-mail communication will rely on unauthenticated and unencrypted SMTP.

To offer protection above these simple communication protocols, there are a number of services that can be utilised within the UAs such that the content of the e-mail (the message body) can be protected against both disclosure and modification (for example, PGP and S/MIME as discussed in the previous chapter).

These techniques, although perfectly functional, do have a number of limitations and require end-users to modify their e-mail interactions, as well as administrative effort to both set up and maintain a secure e-mail implementation. It is also important to understand that although the majority of e-mail that is sent across the globe is open to abuse, it is unlikely that any individual e-mail will be intercepted and its contents examined due to the sheer number of e-mails travelling through the Internet. It is perhaps better to be aware of the limitations and risks and choose appropriate countermeasures when a specific level of security particularly is required.

Takeaways

➤ Be aware of the inherent weaknesses of email protocols and provide additional protection accordingly. For example, ensure firewall restrictions protect vulnerable e-mail communication protocols.

➤ Educate users over the vulnerabilities facing email messages.

> ➢ Educate users to choose the most appropriate means of communication for a message.

> ➢ Unless you have the ability to encrypt end-to-end communication, assume that messages leaving the organisation can be seen and even altered by third parties.

> ➢ Ensure employees are aware of web browser security functionality, and in particular are familiar with the certificate warnings (and their implications) in their chosen browser.

CHAPTER 5: SERVER SIDE SECURITY

This chapter considers the risks faced by e-mail servers at all levels, from organisational servers through mail relays to the recipient's server. Threats to confidentiality, integrity and availability are considered as well as a range of technical countermeasures to detect, prevent or minimise the impact of an attack. Specific attention is given to solutions to mitigate malware, spam and phishing.

Although Chapter 3 introduced a number of countermeasures that can be deployed within the client, the majority of protection is provided at the server end of any e-mail communication. The sections that follow describe a wide range of techniques that can be used on the mail server to protect recipients from malware and Unsolicited Bulk E-mail (UBE), as well as preventing organisational systems being used as the source of UBE.

Firewalls

The first level of protection for an organisation is perhaps the simplest – a typical firewall can offer a good level of protection for the mail server from attacks against the underlying operating system (e.g. Windows Server®, Linux/UNIX®), as well as preventing internal desktop users from misusing the organisation's network to relay UBE messages (intentionally or unintentionally). For example, a compromised host inside the organisation can send millions of UBE messages per day if there is no barrier to prevent outgoing SMTP connections. A simple rule to allow only TCP port 25 connections to/from the mail server(s) will force all SMTP traffic through managed systems (with the option to audit and log all outgoing mail). Any systems (i.e. end-user devices) attempting to forward email directly to external mail servers will be detected and logged by the firewall for further investigation (providing the appropriate level of logging is turned on).

Authenticated access

If an organisation uses SMTP internally for clients to send e-mail, adding mandatory authentication will ensure that malware cannot misuse the internal servers (if coupled with a firewall restriction). This could be further combined with encrypted versions of SMTP/POP3/IMAP – ensuring that authentication credentials cannot be captured from the network.

Connection filtering

Incoming e-mail can be filtered based on a number of criteria. Most mail servers support at least a subset of these (with further options often available via plug-in tools).

Blacklist: A blacklist is used to specifically deny individual Internet Protocol (IP) addresses (or whole subnets) from making a connection directly to the mail server. This can be useful where a known subnet (or individual) has been the source of large volumes of UBE (as is often the case with some ISP subnets). Some caution must be used with blacklisting as it can be easy to deny large sections of the IP address ranges by mistake (e.g. 141.0.0.0/8 rather than 141.163.0.0/16).

Whitelist: A whitelist is the complete opposite, instead listing trusted devices from which connections will be accepted. This is often useful to identify branch offices, parent companies, externally hosted web servers, etc. as trusted sources for e-mail. Note that some mail systems may exclude whitelisted source addresses from further filtering.

Greylist: A greylist is a relatively new concept, utilising the 451 SMTP error code (server temporarily not available). When a new e-mail is received by the server, it is initially rejected (451) and a triplet of data is stored (source IP, sender, recipient) with a time stamp. If the sender attempts to resend in less than the preconfigured time limit (often two minutes), the connection is rejected again. Only when the sender delays for more than two minutes will the e-mail be accepted. The concept behind this is quite simple – the vast majority of UBE is sent via botnets (collections of compromised and remotely controlled hosts) and compromised end-user PCs that do not conform to standard SMTP protocol rules. In particular, most

UBE-sending systems do not retry failed connections. As such, greylisting allows legitimate servers (with correctly configured retry cycles) to still send e-mail (albeit with a two-minute delay) while rejecting most UBE. However, it should be noted that very old e-mail clients (and servers) may consider a 451 error code as a permanent failure and not attempt further retries – effectively rendering the destination unreachable. Another problem with greylisting is that if the server retry delay is set too long, users may perceive a delay in the normally instantaneous e-mail delivery.

Host resolving: Another simple filtering mechanism uses the Domain Name System (DNS) Message eXchange (MX) [20] records to determine if the sending host has an appropriate MX entry. Any host acting as a mail server should have a DNS MX entry to be able to provide its own incoming mail service, hence any host attempting to send email without a suitable MX entry cannot receive a Non Delivery Report (NDR) and is likely to be a source of UBE.

Sender Policy Framework (SPF): SPF[21] addresses the problem of source address spoofing by verifying that the incoming e-mail connection is from an approved sender (as determined by the administrator of the sending domain). This is a subtle difference to the host resolving described above in that MX entries are used to define the host that handles *incoming* e-mail while SPF uses a custom DNS entry (SPF record type) to advertise the hosts within an organisation that are allowed to send e-mail.

DNS blocklists: In addition to black/white/grey listing, there are free public services that provide a simple DNS look-up facility against which incoming connections can be validated. One such example is the Spamhaus project, which provides a number of distinct look-up lists including (but not limited to) the:

---

[20] Further details regarding the role of DNS and mail routing are provided in the Appendix.
[21] RFC 4408 'Sender Policy Framework (SPF) for Authorizing Use of Domains in E-Mail, Version 1', 2006, IETF.
http://tools.ietf.org/html/rfc4408 (accessed 1 September 2010)

- Spamhaus Block List (SBL), which contains records of IP addresses reported as being 'involved in the sending, hosting or origination of Unsolicited Bulk Email'; [22]

- Exploits Block List (XBL), which contains records of IP addresses reported as being infected by various forms of malware;

- Policy Block List (PBL), which contains records of IP addresses that the respective administrators have defined as not permitted to send outbound SMTP traffic (for example, ISP customers on dynamic IP addresses or organisational desktop PCs);

- Domain Block List (DBL), which contains records of domains referenced in UBE messages (for example, phishing sites, 419 scams, malware hosting sites).

These services respond to simple DNS look-up requests. As an incoming connection is received, the source IP address of the connection is submitted to the block list provider via DNS (typically) with a simple error code (specific IP addresses usually beginning 127.0.0.x) returned indicating if the submitted IP address exists on the respective block list – this simple process can effectively filter 80%+ of incoming e-mails. [23]

Spamhaus does provide a combined look-up list named ZEN that allows a single query against the SBL, XBL and PBL lists. It should be noted that Spamhaus services are only available for free to low-volume e-mail sites, although a chargeable service is available and similar services can also be obtained from managed security providers.

Address filtering

Although connection filtering will capture the majority of undesired e-mail messages, there is still an opportunity to

---

[22] Spamhaus website, 2010. *www.spamhaus.org/sbl/* (accessed 1 September 2010)

[23] 'Effective Spam Filtering', Spamhaus website, January 2010. *www.spamhaus.org/whitepapers/effective_filtering.html* (accessed 1 September 2010)

undertake further filtering based on the sender and recipient e-mail addresses. These filtering mechanisms allow specific e-mail addresses (or domains) to be allowed or blocked.

Sender filtering: This can be used to block specific senders (or domains) from communicating with the mail server. This can be useful where a specific sender has been repeatedly targeting the organisation's mail accounts (a targeted spear-phishing attack). This can also be used to block blank sender addresses (often used for UBE).

Recipient filtering: This can be used to only accept e-mails addressed to specific recipients (typically for addresses linked to active user accounts). Using this option will ensure that emails addressed to recipients who are not in the organisational e-mail directory will be bounced. As most UBE is addressed to seemingly randomly generated e-mail addresses (e.g. asmith@domain, bsmith@domain, csmith@domain), any UBE that reaches the server is likely to result in high levels of NDRs. Spammers often use these to determine legitimate e-mail addresses for more focused spamming efforts.

Content filtering

Once an e-mail has been processed through the various filtering techniques described in this chapter, there are still further security mechanisms that can be deployed to reduce the risks to an organisation:

Phishing filters: Although the majority of spam mail will be detected through DNS blocklists or greylisting, some UBE will always manage to bypass these mechanisms (especially as new UBE hosts may not appear immediately on blocklists). Additional content-based scanning (often using heuristics) can identify spam-style e-mails (e.g. messages using excessive capitalisation or disguised words, such as p0rn, c1al1is and v1agra).

Anti-virus (AV): as AV scanning is likely to be the most intensive operation compared with the relatively simplistic IP and e-mail address checking, it is best achieved once the other mechanisms have reduced the e-mail volume to more manageable levels. As e-mails are received, the body content (and attachments) can be scanned using a mail server AV solution. Many mail server AV solutions also allow extension filtering (e.g. blocking .exe, .com, .pif, etc.), which can be used to prevent potential malware from reaching the organisation (as well as enforcing organisational policies regarding attachments). It should be noted that decisions need to be made over how to handle encrypted messages and attachments that are non-readable (and hence non-scannable by the AV system).

Keyword filtering: Although less commonly used for direct detection of UBE (having been replaced by heuristically based solutions), keyword filtering can still be useful for policy enforcement. Examples here could include spotting words of an obscene or offensive nature, or flagging e-mails mentioning names of competitors, etc. Keyword filtering has to be used carefully, as some well-intended keywords may generate excessive false positives if not correctly utilised. For example, filtering for the word 'sex' could flag occurrences of 'Essex', 'Sussex', etc., while messages containing the word 'socialism' could be blocked due to the substring 'cialis' (an erectile dysfunction medication frequently advertised in spam messages). Incidents of this nature are often referred to as the 'Scunthorpe problem'. [24]

Challenge/response

It is perhaps unsurprising that, as detection mechanisms have improved, so has the ability of the UBE generators to evade them. In response to this, some administrators have implemented an automated challenge/response system that requires the sender of any e-mail to verify that they are a 'human' in a similar fashion to the use of CAPTCHA (Completely Automated Public Turing test to tell Computers and Humans Apart) mechanisms in websites. On sending an e-mail to a challenge/response-protected server, the recipient receives back an e-mail asking them to confirm that they are indeed human (Figure 15). This is usually achieved through the use of a simple reply to the e-mail (embedding a unique code in

---

[24] McCullagh, D., 'Google's chastity belt too tight', CNET website, 23 April 2004. *http://news.cnet.com/2100-1032 3-5198125.html* (accessed 1 September 2010)

the subject field) or via a unique hyperlink. Such systems usually record the authorised sender for future messages, so that the effort to each sender is minimal. Failing to respond to the challenge and subsequently sending further unauthorised mail usually results in an addition to a blocklist for that particular sender. It should be noted that in Figure 15, clicking reply uses the SMTP REPLY-TO address '*reply_username_B143D1C7-B 7F8-1DDB-00E1 - FFB200861010@domain*'.

Figure 15: Example challenge/response e-mail

E-mail gateway

Although the technologies described so far in this chapter can be integrated into the front-end mail server, there is value in filtering messages before they reach this point. An e-mail gateway (or e-mail proxy service on a firewall) can pre-filter connections and reduce the mail server load by making decisions before forwarding. These systems can often apply multiple levels of filtering, usually implementing blocklists (white, black, grey, DNS) before applying AV and keyword filtering. One potential advantage of this approach is that, if employees are allowed to download personal e-mail from external servers, an e-mail gateway can forcibly scan the messages before reaching the client (hence applying at least some of the organisational e-mail policy) and, therefore, reducing the risks from malware or information disclosure.

Relaying

An open relay is a mail server that is configured to allow external hosts to send e-mail destined for external hosts through it (Figure 16). A correctly configured mail server will only accept e-mail destined for external domains from its own (usually internal) authorised users. To help with this problem, there are a number of open relay testing services (e.g. *www.abuse.net/relay.html*), as well as comprehensive guidance for fixing an open relay server (*www.mail-abuse.%20com/an_sec3rdparty.html*). If an organisation's mail server is detected as an open relay, not only is it likely to be used by third parties to relay UBE (with the potential to send millions of e-mails per day), but it is quite likely that the organisation will be unable to send legitimate e-mails to many external recipients who use blocklists. It is worth noting that an open relay can occur accidentally, as some older mail servers are configured to allow relaying by default, and it is possible that a server can appear without being deliberately installed due to the defaults used by some installations. In order to minimise such risks, it is important that administrators are aware of server installations and routinely check for e-mail traffic originating from non-approved servers.

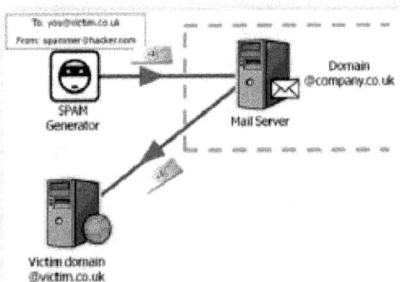

Figure 16: Illustrative example of an open relay

UBE by attachment

As already mentioned, there are problems with filtering encrypted e-mail messages (as they cannot be read by automated filtering systems). However, in recent years, security companies have reported increasing cases of UBE attachments, including MP3 and Portable Document Format (PDF) attachments. These formats (among others) can be more difficult to interpret automatically with organisations often facing the difficult choice of either accepting these file types with no verification of the content, or imposing a blanket file extension block to eliminate the risk. It is inevitable that the use of alternative attachment formats will continue and without appropriate tools to check the content it is advisable to provide training to ensure that staff are able to distinguish legitimate attachments and are able to recognise undesirable content (or at least have a clear mechanism for reporting questionable messages).

Takeaways

➢ Consider the appropriate combination of protection techniques for e-mails. A multi-layered approach (from firewall and filtering through to AV) is likely to be the most effective.

➢ Be aware of the trade-off between strong restrictions on incoming e-mail and the problem of false positives resulting in legitimate e-mails being blocked.

➢ Ensure that mail servers are regularly tested for vulnerabilities.

➢ Have a clear policy on employees accessing and downloading personal e-mails from external servers.

➢ Ensure that users are suitably educated over the nature of e-mail exploits and are able to identify malware, phishing and other exploitative e-mails.

> ➤ Review guidance available from independent bodies (e.g. Center for Internet Security[25] or National Institute of Standards and Technology[26]).

[25] Center for Internet Security. *http://cisecurity.org/* (accessed 1 September 2010)

[26] National Institute of Standards and Technology. *http://csrc.nist.gov/publications/PubsSPs.html* (accessed 1 September 2010)

CHAPTER 6: E-MAIL ARCHIVING

> In addition to conveying individual messages, email also accumulates to become a significant data source in its own right and therefore represents an asset that may be both useful and important to maintain for later reference. This chapter considers the issues surrounding the storage and archiving of organisational e-mail. The discussion encompasses the need to store messages for business purposes, as well as for regulatory requirements, including consideration of evidential value.

Given its importance to business operations, it is relevant to consider how e-mail can be retained for later use. This gives rise to the consideration of how to archive messages in the most effective manner.

A key point to note at the outset is that e-mail archiving is not the same thing as backing up, not least because the motivations are different. While backing up aims to provide a safeguard against some kind of data loss or system failure scenario, archiving provides a route for e-mail retention with the upfront expectation that it will need to be accessed again. So, rather than just being a bulk repository from which data can be recovered, the archive needs to offer a more flexible basis for search and retrieval.

In terms of existing practice, survey findings from MessageLabs have suggested that only 27% of organisations are using a dedicated archiving solution.[27] Meanwhile, 42% take back-ups, 8% simply leave it on the server, and 15% do nothing at all. In spite of these results, the survey (which was based upon responses from 111 e-mail managers) also determined that 65% thought that archiving was important.

---

[27] MessageLabs. 2010. *Email Archiving; Top 10 myths & challenges (& solutions)*. MessageLabs Ltd, Symantec Hosted Services. *www.messagelabs.co.uk/white papers/archiving challenges* (accessed 1 September 2010)

Organisations need to consider archiving for two fundamental reasons: because there is business value to retaining the communications, and because they may face a legal obligation to do so. These perspectives are considered in the sections that follow.

Archiving because we want to

E-mail can provide a vast amount of information about decisions and the context in which they were taken. From this perspective, it can be considered to be a component of the wider corporate memory, and thus a very desirable resource to preserve and reference. For instance, maintaining an archive can help to evidence and explain business decisions, to recover useful contacts that have not been stored in the address book, or to simply find out where things were left when picking up the thread of an old discussion that has not been active for some time. Indeed, referring again to the MessageLabs findings, a variety of reasons were cited for needing to search through old e-mails, with the top three being location of business records (59%), recovery of deleted e-mails (49%), and contributing to an internal human resources investigation (40%).

Although the need to archive may in some cases be driven by internally imposed constraints such as mailbox quotas, it is important to realise that it is not simply a question of being able to hive off older messages to somewhere else and then generally forget about them. A number of potential constraints need to be recognised in terms of storing, searching, protecting and backing up the archive, such that we can get to the contents in a useful way when needed, without exposing it to unauthorised access or the risk of inadvertent loss.

It is also important to consider *what* needs to be archived and how to most effectively handle it. For example, it is clearly undesirable to retain e-mails harbouring spam, phishing and malware, and it would not be optimal to end up storing multiple copies of large attachments just because they have been received by multiple users within the organisation. As such, archiving ideally requires an intelligent approach that minimises this sort of overhead.

If the administration of such a solution cannot be handled in-house, it is worth noting that organisations, such as MessageLabs, offer hosted archiving solutions, which also free client organisations from capacity-related concerns that might arise from the volume of e-mail being handled.

Archiving because we have to

The other perspective on archiving is when we face an obligation to maintain records. Organisations may face such a requirement for a number of legal and regulatory reasons, relating to both core business and accompanying issues such as HR or health and safety. Indeed, referring back to the aforementioned MessageLabs survey, almost a third of the respondents indicated that their archiving activities were motivated by compliance requirements.

The specifics of legal and regulatory demands will vary by geography and jurisdiction, but as an example we can consider relevant legislation from the UK perspective. Here we find two particular Acts of Parliament that carry implications for email archiving, namely the Data Protection Act 1998[28] and the Freedom of Information Act 2000.[29] The key facts about the related laws are as follows.

Data Protection Act 1998

- It applies to organisations in both the private and the public sectors.

- It provides rights for individuals to gain access to personal data (both factual and opinion-based) that is held about them.

- It places obligations on the organisation holding the data to surrender all requested data within 20 days.

---

[28] See
www.opsi.gov.uk/acts/acts1998/ukpga_19980029_en_1
[29] See
www.opsi.gov.uk/Acts/acts2000/ukpga_20000036_en_1

Freedom of Information Act 2000

- It applies to public authorities only.

- It provides rights for persons to be informed in writing whether a public authority holds particular information, and, if so, for a copy of it to be supplied (albeit with some exemptions covering areas such as national security, defence and information provided in confidence).

- Organisations failing to comply can be held in contempt of court and face consequent penalties, including jail.

Considering the practical requirements that these laws place upon organisations, they should raise fundamental questions about whether the organisation would be in a position to respond (i.e. whether it is maintaining the data and is confident in its ability to search it). It is certain that locating data from unstructured back-ups of e-mail potentially spanning several years would present a major challenge, especially given the requirement to locate both facts and opinions about the data subject concerned. As such, a specific and planned archiving strategy would be a valuable step towards reducing the burden (e.g. time and staff effort) when facing the need to comply with a disclosure request.

As a related aside, it should be noted that deleting e-mails in order to avoid the potential to disclose them is not an acceptable approach, and may indeed bring the organisation into conflict with other legal obligations to maintain full and accurate records (for example, relating to personnel and financial issues). Thus, in order to facilitate compliance with the law, organisations require a means of storing e-mails in a manner that is both secure and offers effective retrieval.

A final point to note, given the potential legislative motivations for archiving, is the importance of engaging legal counsel to support the process. The decisions on what to archive should not simply be left to the IT department to decide, as in most cases they are just the custodians (rather than the owners) of the data concerned.

Takeaways

➢ E-mail can provide a valuable source of information for ongoing reference, and so retention measures are required to ensure that it is not lost.

➢ Consider what should be archived and whether a locally managed or a remotely hosted solution would be more effective (e.g. in view of the associated maintenance and capacity demands).

➢ Consider your ability to respond to disclosure requirements. Is e-mail correspondence maintained and held in a form that lends itself to search and retrieval?

➢ Ensure that procedures for searching and recovering information from the archive are established and tested before a genuine need to use them arises.

CHAPTER 7: ETHEREAL E-MAIL

> This chapter briefly considers the increasing popularity of Cloud-based computing and in particular the Software as a Service (SaaS) e-mail model. The discussion presents a brief overview of some of the issues that must be considered when moving to an e-mail solution outside of the traditional corporate network perimeter.

Although running an e-mail system for an organisation may seem a relatively trivial task to some, there are significant challenges to maintaining an efficient and effective service that meets the high expectations of users. With a need to support hardware, software, archiving and backup, and with an increasingly mobile workforce, it is no surprise that more organisations are considering adoption of the 'Cloud' for their business-critical e-mail services.

A move to Cloud-based e-mail services (where email services are provided over the Internet to an organisation by an external provider as a hosted service) is not to be taken lightly, as all the previously mentioned issues will continue to be of concern. By moving to a service model, the physical/practical issues may well be removed (physical storage, back-up, cooling, power, etc.), but the organisation will now have to manage an email platform that is potentially less configurable then an in-house solution.

Some of the key considerations are summarised in the paragraphs that follow.

Security: By moving to a Cloud-based service, organisations can provide an effective solution to the issue of physical location (ensuring that important data is physically isolated from the main organisational sites). This can be further extended by co-locating, using multiple physical locations of Cloud data-centres. When selecting a service provider, it is important to consider issues of isolation from other users (if using a shared service) and the mechanism for *secure* communication between organisational users and the Cloud service.

Responsibility: One of the common concerns when outsourcing e-mail services is the physical location of the e-mail (and any regulatory/legal issues introduced by the specific location). Irrespective of the physical location of the e-mail, the organisation is ultimately responsible for the email messages and must ensure compliance with any legislation in whichever country the messages reside in. It should be noted that some service providers allow customers to choose in which country their data is stored to ensure regulatory compliance (or to avoid specific issues relating to individual countries). The legality of storing and accessing e-mails in a variety of jurisdictions must be considered, as content that is perfectly legal to view and store in one country may be in contravention of local laws in another. Consideration should also be given to security issues in relation to cryptography, as some countries may ban the use of encryption technology, or require organisations to provide access to encrypted content on request.

Support: When selecting an e-mail service provider, it is important to consider the level of support that will accompany it. Moving to an external provider should not be based solely on price, and consideration should be given to a range of factors, including the availability of competent support. It is worth noting that few organisations will have an in-house team of dedicated e-mail support technicians whereas a credible e-mail service provider is likely to offer a substantial support service of specialised professionals.

Mailbox size: Although not an obvious security issue, the availability of virtually unlimited storage may discourage users from properly managing their mailboxes. In particular, users may lose the skill of correctly storing, archiving or deleting emails, instead saving *everything*. Although this may not be seen as a problem by the individual user, Cloud-based cost models may change over time – an organisation with 1,000 users, each with a 100MB mailbox, could easily find itself with 1GB (or even greater) per mailbox very quickly, with potential for incurring excessive costs for storage and back-up. Large mailboxes will also introduce problems for finding important information (for users or organisations), which may have legal implications in contexts such as the freedom of information requests highlighted in Chapter 6.

Takeaways

> Think carefully before moving to an externally hosted e-mail service. Cost savings are only one aspect to be considered.

> Consider legislative/regulatory requirements very carefully, and ensure that you are still able to meet any expected obligations to users, clients, etc.

> Give particular consideration to the implications of storing data in another jurisdiction (both legal and ethical).

CHAPTER 8: RISKING OUR REPUTATION

> In addition to watching what we receive, we also need to be concerned about what gets sent out, with staff misuse of e-mail introducing risks from reputational and legal perspectives. If a message has been sent from a business address, then many recipients will assume that it reflects the views and beliefs of the organisation concerned, which becomes problematic if employees start sending out messages with potentially offensive or legally dubious content. In addition, the ease of onward transmission means that messages can rapidly spread far beyond the originally intended recipient(s). With such risks in mind, this chapter examines some real-life examples and then considers the policy measures that organisations should consider in order to guide and govern acceptable use.

Chapter 2 has already flagged that approximately a quarter of organisations scan their outgoing mail for inappropriate content. One of the fundamental reasons for doing so is to prevent such messages from reflecting badly upon the organisation, potentially tarnishing its image or bringing its name into disrepute. This chapter begins by examining some examples of how this might happen, before proceeding to consider the fact that classifications of what is inappropriate may be a bit of a grey area and that a clear policy is needed to govern this as well as to underpin other aspects of e-mail usage.

Going down in history

For a landmark example, let's consider the case of Claire Swire, which (at the time of writing, almost a decade later) is still a high-ranking result in a Google search for 'infamous emails'! The incident began on 7 December 2000, when Swire e-mailed 10 friends a joke about a sperm bank. In some cases, this alone would have led to trouble for breaching e-mail usage policy, but for Swire things started to go rather more significantly wrong when she replied to one of the recipients (her boyfriend, Bradley Chait).[30] The real problems then began when Chait kindly decided to share this e-mail with six of his friends, changing the message title to something more suggestive. Within three minutes of receiving it, one of these friends had forwarded it to 12 of his contacts, and within a couple of hours the message had spread around the world. Not only had hundreds of people received it directly, but it was also picked up as a story in the international media (with sources as diverse as the *New York Post, Le Monde,* Melbourne's *The Age* and the BBC). The unexpected explosion of the story was doubtless embarrassing at an individual level for Swire, who consequently went into hiding to avoid the media attention. Additionally, the incident was of significant concern to Chait's employer, the international law firm Norton Rose, which found itself named in many of the resulting stories. Indeed, while no long-term reputational damage ensued, the company may still be finding it difficult to escape the association. For example, at the time of writing, a Google search for 'Norton Rose email' still pulls up several references to the incident ahead of any results relating to contact addresses at the company. Perhaps unsurprisingly, Norton Rose was none too pleased that some of its employees had been at the heart of the incident and the forwarding of the messages, and five staff consequently faced disciplinary action for breach of the terms and conditions of their employment.[31]

Another notable case occurred just a few months later, in May 2001, when investment banker Peter Chung began a new job in Seoul with The Carlyle Group. Chung was very happy with his new location and the opportunities it offered him, and used his company e-mail account to send a message to friends back

---

[30] Readers interested in the specifics of the e-mail dialogue can find it online by entering the following address via *www.archive.org* and selecting one of the archived copies:
http://claireswireonline.tripod.com/theemail.htm. Please note that the original page no longer works, and so the archive service needs to be used to recover it.

[31] BBC. 2000. 'Smutty e-mailers keep their jobs', *BBC News Online,* 21 December 2000. *http://news.bbc.co.ukf+1/hi/uk/1081543.stm* (accessed 1 September 2010).

home. Unfortunately, however, in addition to describing the details of his new apartment, Chung explained how he was going to '**** every hot chick in Korea over the next two years' and exploit the hospitality of other bankers ('they pretty much cater to my every whim'). Chung then brought his correspondence to a close by saying 'someone's gotta start FedExing me boxes of condoms, I brought out about forty boxes but I think I'll run out of them by Saturday'. Just as with the Swire case, it was thanks to subsequent forwarding that the message became an Internet incident, with copies still persisting online today.[32] Unfortunately for Chung, his new employers were among those who got to see it, and from a reputational perspective it is easy to see why The Carlyle Group might have had even more of an issue with Peter Chung than Norton Rose had with Bradley Chait. Whereas Chait had simply used the company's e-mail for inappropriate correspondence, Chung had amplified this by also giving an undesirable impression of how he conducted himself in the line of business. With this in mind, it perhaps unsurprising to find that, just two days after sending the message, Chung found himself resigning from the very job he had been bragging about.

Just having a laugh?

If your experience is anything like ours, then you will surely know at least one person who feels obliged to e-mail everyone they know with the latest jokes and amusing images. However, while such mailings may seem fine from an individual perspective, there are some issues that ought to be recognised from the business viewpoint. For example, although jokes may not pose a direct security risk (unless they are used as the trigger to get users to open a message carrying malware), they can still have a tangible impact upon productivity. Indeed, if all the recipients of such a message spend a minute or two to read it, and then possibly some more time to send copies to their

---

[32] At the time of writing a copy can be found at
http://applicant.com/an-email-to-friends-that-ended-a-golden-career/,
but a search for any of the aforementioned quotes should also find it in full.

friends, then it is easy to see how associated time-wasting would amass across the organisation. Moreover, as with general spam, joke messages represent an unnecessary overhead on the mail server and the network. While this may effectively go unnoticed from an internal perspective, there are perhaps greater implications when dealing with mobile users if they are using services that incur data charges by the byte.

Perhaps the biggest issue, however, is the potential for the content of such mailings to cause offence (particularly given the language, imagery, concepts and innuendo that many of them are prone to carrying). Whatever the joke, there is always a chance that it will potentially offend *somebody's* sensibilities. In some cases recipients will be quietly upset and in others they may be loudly offended. Neither scenario is particularly desirable, and so care should ideally be taken to avoid them. If a potentially offensive message was received from someone else within the organisation, then it could lead to a HR issue (involving the grievance and disciplinary procedures respectively). The situation is likely to become more acute with the appearance of legislation, such as the UK Equality Act 2010, which extends new protection to people who feel they have been victimised or harassed. In this context, employers would be advised to directly ban all sharing of smutty and other jokes, in order to avoid accusations of failing to protect their employees. Meanwhile, if one of your people has e-mailed it externally, then it could lead to complaints from recipient organisations.

Of course, you cannot control what people choose to send you, so the judgement call (and advisable policy area) comes in terms of what you ought to be sending to other people. Another point to note here is that very rarely are people just passing on the joke. These messages tend to get forwarded onwards and onwards, with the names, e-mail addresses and signature lines of previous recipients progressively accumulating within the body of the message. As a result, there is potential for employers to get drawn into it, with company names being visible alongside their employees, which is clearly not very welcome if what they are doing is forwarding offensive material and ripe jokes.

Putting it in a policy

Fundamentally, if suitable rules have not been formally recorded somewhere, then trustworthy staff may be legitimately concerned about what they can do, while those seeking to misbehave are handed an easy excuse to claim that they did not know any better. As such, it is important to establish a clear policy to govern e-mail activity and acceptable use.

There are a variety of points that such a policy needs to address, and some key considerations are summarised in the pages that follow.

Attachments

Given the clear potential to carry malware, users should be given specific guidance in relation to the handling of attachments.

Incoming attachments should be regarded with caution in order to reduce the risk of malware infection. Users should be made aware that scripts and executable content are particularly notable in this context, but that other file types cannot be guaranteed to be risk-free. Additionally, the advice should highlight that, although they are by no means the only source of problems, attachments received from unknown sources, or unexpectedly from legitimate contacts, should be regarded with particular suspicion.

The policy should also address outgoing messages, and users should be made aware that they must be careful not to pass on malware or other inappropriate attachments to others.

More generally, users should be made aware that even if they are able to attach certain materials, it does not guarantee that their intended recipients will be able to receive them (e.g. on the basis that large attachments and/or particular file types may be blocked at the remote end).

Appropriateness of outgoing content

In contrast to being wary of malware and other malicious threats, this point relates to content that users may intentionally place within their messages. There are a number of perspectives that users ought to be made aware of, and they ought to be clearly advised to avoid including content (in message bodies or attachments) that may:

- be in breach of legislation (e.g. data protection or copyright);

- compromise the confidentiality of the organisation;

- be reputationally damaging to the organisation;

- potentially cause distress, harm, nuisance or offence to recipients.

The policy ought to include specific caution against the inclusion of any of the following within e-mail communications:

- pornographic, paedophilic or other obscene material;

- sexist, racist and other discriminatory content;

- material that could be construed as defamatory, libellous or threatening.

Users should also be advised against sending any messages that purport to represent their organisation or another individual without appropriate authorisation.

Uncontrolled incoming content

Users should be made aware that some aspects of incoming content will be beyond the organisation's control and that they may consequently find themselves in receipt of unwanted messages containing explicit or offensive content. Although technical measures can certainly be employed to reduce the problem (e.g. via spam filtering and malware scanning), there is still the potential for things to get through, and so, in order to avoid unwarranted complaints from users, the policy should make it clear that the organisation cannot accept responsibility for what is received.

Users can, however, be encouraged to report such unwanted messages to an appropriate point of contact *(see below),* which may ease their concern and potentially provide the organisation with intelligence to improve any e-mail filtering controls. Actively encouraging such reports will be particularly important for illegal content or messages that appear to be specifically targeting the organisation in some way (e.g. spear phishing of employees).

Personal use of e-mail

This is an area in which there is likely to be significant scope for variation between organisations, with some of the possible broad scenarios including:

- permitted on the proviso that it does not conflict with performance of work duties;

- permitted but with a requirement that personal messages are explicitly marked as such in the subject line;

- permitted only for emergency situations;

- not permitted under any circumstance.

Whatever the case, the key point is that the statement must be clear and unambiguous to staff, and any bounds should be properly defined.

Bulk mailing

Another factor relating to appropriateness of use, this seeks to prevent inconvenience to other users through receipt of unwanted messages, as well as complaints back to the organisation regarding the misuse of its facilities.

In providing a policy for mass mailings, it is relevant to define a threshold of what it means (e.g. sending to more than 100 recipients), and to clarify that this applies to internal messaging as well as to the outside world. Repeated messaging of the same or similar content could also qualify.

One question that might help people to consider whether someone else *really* needs to be in a recipient list is to ask themselves whether they would also make the effort to send that person a copy if it was being done on paper. Genuine application of this question can help to cut down recipient lists considerably. Highlighting that the impacts of bulk mailing may include wasted time and inconvenience to other users (particularly if receipt of unwanted mail was to cause their mailbox to become full, and thus potentially prevent them from performing other tasks) can also help users to identify with the problem.

Point(s) of contact for queries and reporting of abuse

Given the importance of e-mail to the organisation, users will require a clear route for addressing any queries and problems that may arise. For example, having a point of contact will become relevant to users if:

- their e-mail is not working;

- they believe that they have received a virus or other malware;

- they encounter targeted phishing attacks or other dubious messages.

The typical approach here is to have a 'postmaster' address (i.e. postmaster@xyz-organisation.com) as a single point of contact for all queries and reports. In many cases the handling of messages sent to this address is likely to be wrapped into the wider IT support function, but the potential criticality of e-mail may mean that handling related incidents needs to be prioritised over some IT support issues.

Compliance requirements

Staff in many organisations, particularly those in the public sector, can also find themselves needing to abide by acceptable use policies from governing bodies. For example, in the UK, bodies such as the National Health Service (NHS) (for the healthcare domain) and JANET (for further and higher education) have umbrella policies that apply to all of the underlying organisations within their sectors. Additionally, there will be a need for usage to comply within any relevant national legislation from the country involved. Ideally, however, rather than expecting individuals to consult multiple sources, it is advisable for the key principles to be embodied within a single policy from their direct employer.

Usage monitoring and e-mail access by the organisation

Users should be made aware that the organisation has the right to monitor e-mail usage for a number of reasons, including prevention of misuse, investigation of potential incidents, evidencing business transactions, and general performance monitoring and maintenance activities. The guidance should highlight that in some circumstances this may involve the actual content of messages being seen by those conducting the activities. It is relevant to highlight that users themselves will stand to benefit from the monitoring, as it will help the organisation to protect them against malicious threats and the implications of misuse by other users.

The policy should also identify that there may be circumstances in which a user's account needs to be accessed in their absence (e.g. if they are ill or out of contact) in order to fulfil business obligations.

If encrypted mail is used, users should be made aware that there may still be a requirement (and indeed a potential legal obligation) to provide decryption keys in some circumstances.

Takeaways

➢ Ensure that users are made aware that any emails they send out from their work account has the potential to reflect upon the organisation as well.

➢ Include a standard disclaimer within messages to explicitly signify that the views expressed are those of the author and are not necessarily endorsed by the organisation.

➢ Ensure the establishment, promotion and enforcement of a comprehensive e-mail usage policy, addressing at least the key areas flagged in this chapter.

APPENDIX: ADDITIONAL NOTES

This section contains brief additional notes to support earlier chapters. While the information is not essential reading, it may be of interest to readers requiring more detail of the technologies that help to support e-mail.

Domain Name System (DNS)

It is worth noting that the DNS plays a role in the security of an e-mail system. E-mail forwarding relies on DNS MX entries, which determine which IP address (or addresses) handle incoming e-mail for a specific domain. For example, the microsoft.com domain has the MX entries shown in Figure A1. If an attacker is able to control the DNS MX entries either directly or through a DNS cache poisoning attack,[33] it is possible to either divert e-mail or block incoming mail to a specific server.

Figure A1: Example MX entries for a domain

DomainKeys

DomainKeys is a relatively recent technique (2007) that can be used to verify the source and content of an e-mail using digital signatures and DNS domain records. DomainKeys was superseded by DomainKeys Identified Mail (DKIM) as a Request For Comments (RFC) standard.[34] The use of DKIM allows a recipient

---

[33] United States Computer Emergency Readiness Team (US-CERT). 2008. 'Vulnerability Note VU#800113, Multiple DNS implementations vulnerable to cache poisoning'. *www.kb.cert.org/vuls/id/800113* (accessed 1 September 2010)

[34] RFC 4871 'DomainKeys Identified Mail (DKIM) Signatures', 2007, IETF.

to verify that the claimed sender domain is the genuine source of the e-mail, as well as validating that the e-mail content has not been modified. It is worth noting that relatively few e-mail sources are likely to use DKIM; as such, e-mail without a DKIM signature should not be rejected outright, but, instead, fed through other anti-spam systems to prevent false-rejections.

Architectures

Most e-mail is transferred by Message Transfer Agents (MTAs) initially from a local UA. The UA is typically a mail client (e.g. Microsoft® Office Outlook®, Mozilla® Thunderbird®, Microsoft® Entourage®) and transfers messages to an organisational mail server that acts as a Relay MTA. Relay MTAs apply rules to determine how a message should be forwarded, with most messages simply forwarded on to the appropriate mail server for the mail recipient. Figure A2 shows an example route for a simple connection from a local UA to a recipient (indicating typical protocols).

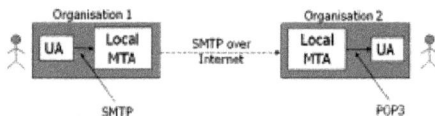

Figure A2: An example e-mail session (simple UA to MTA to MTA to UA)

In Figure A2, the e-mail is sent by the UA in Organisation 1 from the local client to the organisational mail server. This is the first stage of the simple SMTP journey and is likely to remain inside the organisation's boundary and hence still be governed by the appropriate security controls. Once the e-mail leaves the organisation (for delivery to the MTA in Organisation 2), it is likely to be routed through the Internet using simple SMTP, and hence be fully readable to any device through which it travels. On arrival at Organisation 2, the message is stored in the local

MTA ready for the recipient's UA to download the e-mail (traditionally via POP3).

http://tools.ietf.ors/html/rfc4871, (accessed 1 September 2010)

A more complex variation introduces Relay MTAs – this is commonly found in small- and medium-sized enterprises where a local mail server will store e-mails and then forward them to an ISP's mail server for onward forwarding, as illustrated in Figure A3. Note that this model also applies where an organisation outsources e-mail security to a managed security provider.

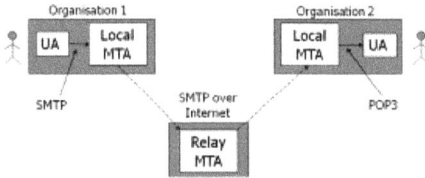

Figure A3: An example e-mail session with a Relay MTA

Additional Secure Sockets Layer (SSL) certificate warning examples

Figures A4 to A6 present some additional examples of browser certificate warnings in order to complement the Mozilla® Firefox® and Microsoft® Internet Explorer® versions presented in Chapter 4.

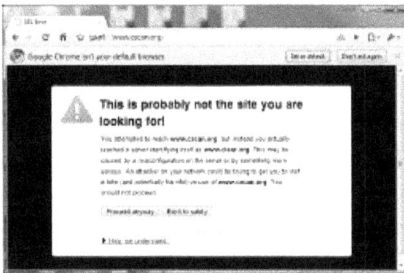

Figure A4: Security certificate warning in Google Chrome v5

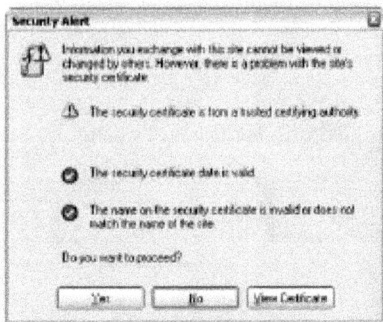

**Figure A5: Security certificate warning in Miocrosoft®
Internet Explorer® 6**

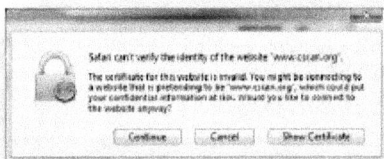

Figure A6: Security certificate warning in Apple® Safari v5

Putting it all together

Although there is no one-size-fits-all recommended approach,
Figure A7 shows how the techniques described in this guide can be
combined to create a secure e-mail architecture.

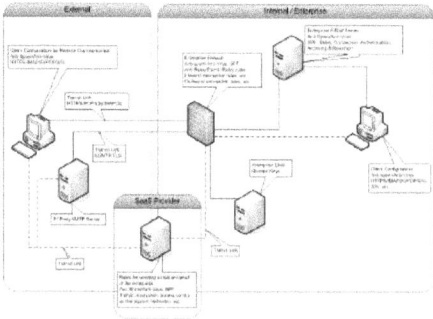

Figure A7: Example secure e-mail architecture
Source: Jayson Agagnier, CISSP. Reproduced with grateful permission.

ITG RESOURCES

IT Governance Ltd. sources, creates and delivers products and services to meet the real-world, evolving IT governance needs of today's organisations, directors, managers and practitioners. The ITG website (*www.itgovernance.co.uk/*) is the international one-stop-shop for corporate and IT governance information, advice, guidance, books, tools, training and consultancy.

www.itgovernance.co.uk/keep-safe-online.aspx is the information page on our website for our online security products resources.

Other Websites

Books and tools published by IT Governance Publishing (ITGP) are available from all business booksellers and are also immediately available from the following websites:

www.itgovernance.co.uk/catalog/355 provides information and online purchasing facilities for every currently available book published by ITGP.

www.itgovernanceusa.com is a US$-based website that delivers the full range of IT Governance products to North America, and ships from within the continental US.

www.itgovernanceasia.com provides a selected range of ITGP products specifically for customers in South Asia.

www.27001.com is the IT Governance Ltd. website that deals specifically with information security management, and ships from within the continental US.

Pocket Guides

For full details of the entire range of pocket guides, simply follow the links at *www.itgovernance.co.uk/publishing.aspx*.

Toolkits

ITG's unique range of toolkits includes the IT Governance Framework Toolkit, which contains all the tools and guidance that you will need in order to develop and implement an appropriate IT governance framework for your organisation. Full details can be found at *www.itgovernance.co.uk/%20products/519*.

For a free paper on how to use the proprietary Calder-Moir IT Governance Framework, and for a free trial version of the toolkit, see *www.itgovernance.co.uk/calder%20moir.aspx*.

There is also a wide range of toolkits to simplify implementation of management systems, such as an ISO/IEC 27001 ISMS or a BS25999 BCMS, and these can all be viewed and purchased online at: *www.itgovernance.co.uk/catalog/1*.

Best Practice Reports

ITG's range of Best Practice Reports is now at *www.itgovernance.co.uk/best-practice-reports.aspx*. These offer you essential, pertinent, expertly researched information on an increasing number of key issues including Web 2.0 and Green IT.

Training and Consultancy

IT Governance also offers training and consultancy services across the entire spectrum of disciplines in the information governance arena. Details of training courses can be accessed at *www.itgovernance.co.uk/training.aspx* and descriptions of our consultancy services can be found at *http://www.itsovernance.co.uk/consultins.aspx*. Why not contact us to see how swe could help you and your organisation?

Newsletter

IT governance is one of the hottest topics in business today, not least because it is also the fastest moving, so what better way to keep up than by subscribing to ITG's free monthly newsletter *Sentinel?* It provides monthly updates and resources across the whole spectrum of IT governance subject matter, including risk management, information security, ITIL and IT service management, project governance, compliance and so much more. Subscribe for your free copy at: *www.itsovernance.co.uk/newsletter.aspx*.

EU for product safety is Stephen Evans, The Mill Enterprise Hub, Stagreenan, Drogheda, Co. Louth, A92 CD3D, Ireland. (servicecentre@itgovernance.eu)